I'M ALL OVER THE PLACE

A BOOK OF
POEMS + PRAYERS + WONDERINGS
BY TANNER OLSON

I'M ALL OVER THE PLACE
A BOOK OF POEMS + PRAYERS + WONDERINGS

Copyright © 2019 by Tanner Olson

ISBN **978-0-578-50977-8**

Illustration *Sarah Solinski*
Photo *Adam Fricke*
Design *Katherine Begalke*

'Welcome!', 'To', 'The', 'Other', and 'Side' are from the recorded album *Welcome to the Other Side* by Written to Speak. They are available to listen to wherever you listen to music.

'Some Days', 'King David', 'Trees', 'Letter', 'Empty Morning', 'Mountain', 'Speak Up / Listen Up' are from the recorded album *All Things* by Written to Speak.

'Two Words', 'Dear You', and 'For Us' are from the recorded album *honest thoughts.* by Written to Speak.

SWORD & SWAN
MEDIA HOUSE

ENDORSEMENTS //

Poetry, the ability to imagine something new and eloquently articulate the results is a gift we could desperately use in our culture right now. I'm glad Tanner reports his findings, helping us see what's unseen in this brave little book.

CJ Casciotta *Author of Get Weird: Discover the Surprising Secret to Making a Difference*

....

At a time when so much emphasis is placed on the hustle and grind, Tanner's words are a beautiful shift. *I'm All Over The Place* will help you come face-to-face with who you really are – a human being, not a human doing.

Alex Lewis Speaker, Writer, and Founder of Car Window Poetry

....

There is real life and real grace in this book of poetry. Tanner's work has been to me a beacon of hope, a call to repentance, and a beckoning home.

Abi Tesfaye Musician & Speaker

....

Tanner's poems are wise yet relevant, quirky yet deep, and fun yet meaningful. His words speak hope into a world longing for more of it.

Kyle Willkom Author, Speaker, and Comedic Rapper

....

Technology has given us unlimited access to information. But what we long for in our day is inspiration. Poetry has this potential, to point beyond data to truth and meaning. Thank you, Tanner, for words that are heartfelt, vulnerable, and human. Thanks for taking us beyond information, to faith and love.

Jeff Cloeter Pastor and Author of, *Loved + Sent*

I'm All Over the Place takes black words on a white page and paints pictures that will create an explosion of colors in your mind. With stunning honesty Tanner Olson reveals the deepest depths of his soul. As you get to know Tanner better through the poems in this book, you will also get to know yourself better. More importantly, you will get to know better the God who showers down abundant grace and peace in Jesus Christ.

Tom Eggebrecht Pastor and Author of, *Fully + Creatively Alive*

....

Poets and artists are essential in speaking to a generation that is overwhelmed by content, conflict, and right answers. Tanner is such an artist. He is not afraid to be messy and vulnerable and even uncertain. He's not afraid to pour out a page of honest thoughts and mixed up feelings. What he brings in this book is an opportunity for others to wonder alongside him, to be assured that they are not the only one, and to be inspired to slow down and consider all that is true and all that is beyond our comprehension.

Leah Abel Ministry Facilitator and Director of Christian Education

....

I WROTE THIS FOR YOU

PART I // BEGIN

PART II // WANDER

PART III // CONTINUE

FOREWARD //

As I sat down to write this foreword I knew I needed some Tanner Olson approved inspiration in my earbuds. But, I found myself torn. Do I opt for Florida based pop-punk outfit New Found Glory? Or, Florida based post-hardcore band Underoath? I decided to split the difference and listen to Underoath's most recent album and New Found Glory's first album. Which got me thinking, for being a place where Americans go to die, Florida sure exports a lot of talent.

Tanner Olson is no exception.

I first met Tanner in the summer of 2009. We were both working at a summer camp in Northern Wisconsin. It is not an understatement to say that his bronze skin, skinny jeans, and screamo band t-shirts made him stick out more than a little bit amidst the flannel and Carhartt of the North Woods. And yet, that summer it was precisely Tanner's unique qualities that endeared him to a culture different than his own, including a seminarian from North Detroit.

It's been nearly a decade since our friendship began, since then Tanner and I have had many adventures. We've spoken alongside each other in coffee shops, hotel conference rooms, and juvenile detention centers. I got to marry him to a brilliant woman inside a skatepark in Nashville. Soon he'll be the godfather to my third-born child. And today I get to write the foreword to his first book.

Here's why this book matters.

The artist Takashi Murakami has famously labeled contemporary Japanese culture as Superflat. Murakami coined this description because he sees in his culture a people that are visually stimulated but spiritually hollow. Amidst an abundance of consumer choices, technological advances, and a constant stream of entertainment (pun intended) there is no depth.

I'm not qualified to comment on Japanese culture. But it's no stretch to label much of life in twenty-first century America as Superflat. The existential questions that humanity has pondered over for millennia are now shoved to the back of our minds so we can remodel our kitchens, scroll through Instagram, or binge watch *Stranger Things* again.

This book is an antidote to anyone seeking to find life beneath the veneer of our contemporary culture.

I can already hear the pushback. "How can a little book of poems be any part of an antidote to our Superflat reality?" And to be fair, this book probably won't change the world. However, in his sweeping review of history, Arnold Toynbee makes the case that civilizations are changed by creative minorities. These are people who find solutions to challenges and inspire others to follow their innovative lead. *I'm All Over the Place* is part of the solution to the flatness of existence that so many of us sense. The pages of this book contain an innovative approach to war against a surface level existence.

Through creative turns of phrase, humor, self-deprecation, and above all honest words of love, Tanner invites the reader to join him in wrestling through questions of life, meaning, and faith. Tanner's words burrow a hole through our cultural malaise and give the reader an opportunity to seek truth and find hope.

Read this book, and don't expect to remain the same.

Read this book and find a world in which things as simple as milkshakes and as complex as love are both saturated in meaning.

Read this book and get ready to see the world as a place enchanted by the One who created it all.

Welcome to the other side.

Grace and peace,

Gabe Kasper
Pastor, University Lutheran Chapel Ann Arbor, MI

INTRODUCTION //

The summer between third and fourth grade I woke each morning to watch Space Jam on our oversized box shaped television in the living room. I popped the tape into the VCR and for the next 100 minutes I watched Michael Jordan and the Looney Tunes take on the Monstars from Moron Mountain. With a basketball in my hands I'd mimic every move as I sang off key to I Believe I Can Fly.

And for a moment, I believed I could.

After Michael Jordan jumped from the free-throw line, dunking to defeat the Monstars and win back his friends' talents (spoiler alert), I'd put on my Nikes and shoot hoops beneath the blazing Florida sun until it disappeared for the night.

There was no question in my mind that I was going to be like MJ.

I felt most alive with a basketball in my hands. On the basketball court there was this unshakeable freedom, a collision of beauty and wholeness that held opportunity for something magical to take place. Basketball is like a blank page as it anticipates a story to be written, a place where anything could become.

In middle school I stood at the free-throw line with less than a second left on the clock. The game was tied and I needed to make one free-throw for us to win the game.
Nerves swarmed in my stomach like an army of bees as I felt every pair of eyes on me.
Even the cute cheerleaders.
Especially the cute cheerleaders.
The referee bounced the ball to me as I began to channel my inner Michael Jordan.
Sweat dripped from my forehead as I tried to slow myself down, taking a deep breath, exhaling nerves.
I dreamed of hitting this shot thousands of times, practicing it daily in our front yard.
I bounced the ball three times before spinning it in my hands, just like MJ. As the ball spun on my fingers I could feel every raised ridge of the leather. Before I bounced the ball again I heard my mom exclaim from the bleachers, "Take your time!"

Thanks mom.

Even if it was the wrong time, this is what I needed to hear.

And recently I've been needing to hear the things I know to be true.

I was in middle school 15 years ago and soon after stepping foot into high school did my dream of becoming a professional basketball player walk out the other side. Setbacks, surgeries, and topping out at 5'10" helped bring this dream to its unfortunate end. When you let go of a dream, something inside of you dies and with mourning and setback comes questions and uncertainty.

And with questions and uncertainty come lies.
Fake truths begin to blend themselves into our thinking, infiltrating our lives and we slowly come to believe them.

That we aren't enough. Or worthy. Or capable.
That we don't matter. And no one will miss us if we are gone.

I've come to learn the truth is easier to believe when all is fine, but once struggle or setback enters the picture, lies become louder and the truth becomes difficult to believe.
Or remember.
Or hold on to.
We begin to distance ourselves from the truth we believe and instead draw closer to the lies, to the great fear welling within.
And fear does a wonderful job of silencing the truth.
And when the truth is silenced, questions begin to weigh heavy.
And uncertainty begins to cloud certainty.
And doubt places distance between who I am and who I want to become.
That's why I started writing.
A blank page became my basketball court, a place where I came alive, writing myself back to life, finding hope in the heaviness of life.

With a pen in my hand I began to believe once again that I could fly, scribbling myself back to life with honesty and hopefulness. I was able to find beauty in the mundane, coming alive like I did on the basketball court. I learned how to wrestle with the noise and how to seek the

silence; to fight the constant chaos and learn how to "take my time."
In my head, I'm all over the place, but writing kept me from going over
the edge, from scribbling a final goodbye. Writing has reminded me this
is all worth living for, the same reminder basketball gave me. The same
freedom I found in basketball, I found in writing. Day after day and page
after page I found myself searching and sifting through poems, prayers,
and wonderings.

And that's exactly what this book is full of: poems, prayers, and
wonderings.

I hope you enjoy.

Much love,

Tanner

Nick!

I'M ALL OVER
THE PLACE

SPREAD HOPE!

A BOOK OF
POEMS + PRAYERS + WONDERINGS
BY TANNER OLSON

POETRY CAN BE

WEIRD AND UNCOMFORTABLE

BUT WHAT IF WE

NEED TO GET

WEIRD AND UNCOMFORTABLE?

- Tanner Olson

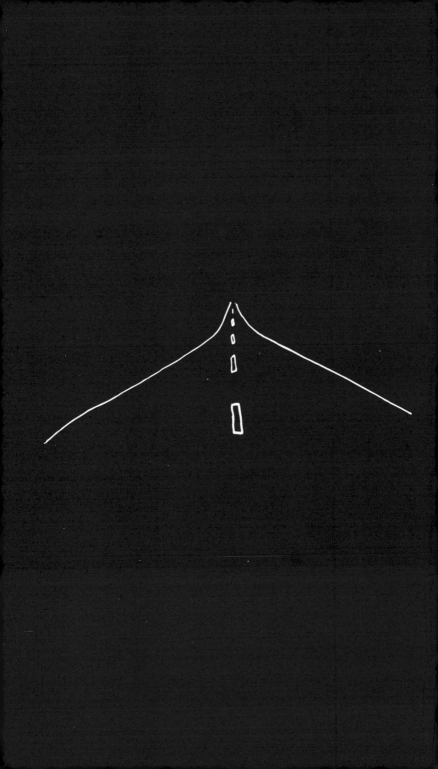

WELCOME //

I'm aware this is most likely your first time hearing me.
Hello.
I grew up down south among the palm trees with Mickey Mouse and a basketball hoop in front of our house.
I wanted to be Michael Jordan until I was 13 and, to this day, *Space Jam* is the greatest movie these blue eyes have ever seen.
I'd rather have a cheeseburger than fame,
and most days I'm called the wrong name.

I'm the second son of my father, I stand four inches taller than my mother, my hero is my brother.
Late one December, I said, "I do," to a grace-filled goddess with eyes so beautiful they could shrink giants.
And late last night I was sent a GIF while half asleep next to the other whole of me.
She couldn't see me giggling under the sheets as I watched a dog run into a glass door over and over and over and over. We've talked about getting a dog of our own.
And we will name him Pancake.

And I still have a hard time being present because I'm stuck in the past and fixed on the future.
I don't know what it's like to live with no regrets or without dreams.
And I write poetry because I can't sing and when I dance it looks like I'm trying to kill a bee without getting stung.

I read these words from a notebook because I cannot memorize,
but I have become mesmerized by how ink changes a page.

I'm no Whitman or Poe, Dickinson or Angelou, Weezy or Swift.

But I write to remain, putting the pen to the paper to keep from causing a ripple and rift.

Writing: the cheapest form of therapy.
Saving my pockets' singles and dimes so I can buy coffee to fuel this dream, sipping myself closer to clarity.

And I'm chasing the heels of 30 and I thought I'd have life figured out

by now, but
I've got more questions than answers.
And all my answers create fresh questions, a constant give and take, a swirling surrounding the pounding within.
Yet, locked within, faith outweighs both, stretching me closer to forever, a restful peace growing beyond the deep.

And deep down inside, hope pumps through my veins, coursing creativity, causing a landslide of possibilities, reminding me it is better to be here together than to leave alone.

And I've been someone I haven't liked, but for all I don't know,
I know grace kills guilt, grabbing my hand, leading me to a blank page to write with freedom and New Found Glory.

I don't have all the right words to write or say, but I've got a lot of words to say.
Some days I think I say too much, but most days I think I think too much.

Over-thinking:
A constant moving within, the shaking and shifting of thoughts, getting myself lost within what ifs, mixing myself up with mix-tapes of mess ups, replaying the wreckage of memories I've tried to lay to rest.
And I'm second guessing what I know to be true, and I know I don't know much but I've come to know kindness isn't overrated and telling you that donuts are delicious is an understatement.
I know I don't want to die with my eyes on a screen or get stuck some-where in between hate and greed.
I know our greatest response is often silence, and if you're quiet enough, you might be able to spread it.

But I also know if something is beautiful, we should speak it.

I know weird and wonderful have more in common than just the W.
And I know learning takes patience and patience takes learning.
I know there is no shame in surrendering and I believe humility requires community.
And community is why we push through to the other side.

And I know two of the sweetest words are "Welcome home".

Welcome.
Home.
Well, come home and we will welcome you with arms and smiles wide.
Well, come home and we will wash the dust from your feet and give you something to eat.
Well, come home, we've been waiting for you.

Welcome home.

LESS //

when i feel like
i am
less
i remember
You aren't afraid
of this
mess

ME TO YOU //

it's bringing
all of me
to all of You
only to hear
"you are
welcome
here."

TO //

Somewhere is everywhere to someone.
And someone is somewhere to someone else.
And I've been someone somewhere for too long,
And everywhere seems to be where I've been lately.

I'm all over the place, confusing myself as I drift in and out of space,
stretching to put some space between the place I've left to leave
behind.

Sometimes growth feels like two steps back, and sometimes flourish-
ing feels like failing.
And I feel like I'm always falling, complicated and calling,
trying to take two steps away from failing.

And Something more is out there.
And that's where I am going.

I'll
escape to explore,
retreat to restore,
be to belong,
And reach the other side of all that is going wrong.

I will continue to wander and wonder within all that is His.
To seek the silence in the solitude.
To create in the chaos.
And give grace to the grave places in my life.
I'm beginning to see more clearly.

Like, in all that is heavy, there is hope.

And as I go,

I will lock hand and hand with knees to the floor, faith to continue,
wake to walk through the front door.
I will keep going to arrive.
I'll crawl out from underneath these concrete sheets and step beyond
this bed into the uncertain and unknown.

Life is calling and I'm answering, and I want to respond with peace in a world shouting dark, cold winds.
I'll sing and lift a sail high, and I'll adventure to find out why.

And I'll reach the other side.

You'll find me beyond the swollen smoke sharing secrets and stories of life and death and what failed to get the best.
You'll find me where it's clear and cloudy with the change I left behind and all my rough-draft letters home.
You'll find me surrounded,
Shoulder to shoulder with the souls who stood close as we stepped together.

We go together to the other side.

Always together.

Never alone.

BEAUTY //

slow me down to see
the beauty of a
new beginning

still me to
forever remember
the beauty
of
not knowing

silent me and speak of
the beauty of
Believing

beauty is
what you placed
in
me.

SLOW //

stop to breathe it in

close your eyes
and do it again

and maybe one day

we'll come to see
slow
is a better way of
living

KING DAVID //

Born to be more than I'll ever understand,
Rushed upon by the Spirit, my story began.
I stood tall in the shadow of a giant to see him fall.
I stepped up to throw and his end was the start of it all.
A slung stone led to a life of battle and rhymes.

Well,
I am a warrior; a writer.
A double-edged sword dueling blade and ink, constructing a life
reflecting smeared reds, broken blues,
the brush grasped by the painter, the Spirit, daily mixing hues.
Sparking saturation, shading with space, tinting with time, creating a
painted picture of God and man intertwined.
And inside the frame my breathing, my being, foreshadowed a time I
never breathed to see,
but a life that saved us all from our breathing.
Our relationship tested, tried, and over time He wrote over,
opening wide my calloused eyes.
Clearing them to see clearly, and I've seen everything.
I've looked deep into life and death
I've seen blood spilt, and tipped over the cup with my own hand.
I've lit fires, sparked separation, and trampled hearts as my enemies
trampled mine while I chased my conscience,
gripping guilt, with death chasing close behind.
I've gazed upon the glorious, witnessing God stand victorious.
And each night, I've stared towards the up all night silent sky with
burning breaths and tear filled eyes.
Inhaling wonder, exhaling the same question that keeps me from sleep:

Who am I?

....

God, I'm just as broken as those that bow.
I'm just as lost as those who haven't been found
I've got mistakes stacked to the top of Your city's walls, but You built
this city and know it as You know me.
But for all I doubt, for all I call out, You chose me.

I am a King.

Or at least that's what they call me,
who Samuel anointed me to be.
But I'm nothing more than a shepherd with lost sheep.
A king with a kingdom, a captain steering a ship sinking.
This drowning vessel, this man I am,
has been scorched and torn by waves unseen.
Ripping sails, rusting nails,
a royal example rotten from regrets, crying unclean.
Tattered boards sinking to Your ocean's floor
These hinges creak, my faults make them cringe and moan

God, I am alone!
And I've amounted to nothing more than strength turned weak.
Shipwrecked I'm still searching for peace to carry me,
for You to hold me!
Because for all I have, all I've wanted is peace,
All I've wanted is for someone to hold me.
My soul burns at both ends seeking salvation, seeking an end, but
both sides of me are drowning by death and dying when all I wanted
is peace!
I spent nights writing, days fighting,
but nothing but patience in Your presence brought peace.
And I searched for peace in the arms of a wife,
in the blood of her man,

I swung for it with a sword in my hands,
burying hearts in Your sand.

I screamed for peace in dirt covered caves, crying out day and night
tossing prayers like seeds to the ground, helpless and hopeful, each
word hit Your dirt,
and You heard my plea, watered my seed.
For the darkness turns to light,
the very way You turn lives from dead to alive.
And now I'm talking in circles,
a struggle to speak straight.
I talk the way I walk.
Stepping a crooked line trying to live aligned with God, to lead mankind,
but even a crooked rod can draw a straight line.

Conviction and reconciliation wrestle inside my mind, and I know grace is alive, and this wound is on the mend,
but God, when will this come to an end?
This life, this valley reeks of death: am I dying?

When will all my questions, my regrets, my sins, these enemies that swirl in the silence of the loudest sound, You've dealt with them, but when will this end?
You made haste, stepped into my place, extending grace.
You call me your Beloved,
And Hallelujah, You do not deal with us according to our stain, nor repay us according to our ways.
For all my hand writes, for all my mind composes, You work in a way man cannot understand, You answer who I am.
Your hand placed all things under our feet, holding us as we seek, as we speak, as we sink, pleading for You to save the weak.
And for as often as I ask who am I, You tell me –
You help me understand.

And, bless You, bless the Lord, oh my soul, You are with me.
And shouldn't that be enough for me?
I'll live with this mess I am.
Redemption is part of Your plan.
I may never see me as You do, but I know You see me, I know You hear me, I know You are with me, and that makes me Yours.
I am Yours.
You've brought me this far, and I am just a speck in your eye, another life this side of the light,
But You are with me, through all my questioning, You are with me.

God you comfort me when I stare into the dark eyes of enemies.
And You tell me goodness is right behind me and mercy follows closer.

....

Well, get me there.
Take me there.
I will build You a house,
Magnify Your name forever, and surrender all of this for all of You.
May all of this be for all of You.

....

Forever.

TWO WORDS //

Two words changed it all.
They found my lost life, located my misplaced eyes—fixing them on where they should have always been.
They flipped my upside-down life right-side-up as I stood to the One we've been waiting for.
I breathed new life as my old self unexpectedly died.
But before all this saving, I lived a life of stumbling.
And somewhere along this crooked road, I wound up face down in the footprints of unforgiving men.

I wasn't able to find my footing when I fell
And I felt like I was falling.
God, I was falling.

You see,
These hands tingled copper-fit fingers that reached for filthy silver from empty pockets.
I took from the hands that had nothing and placed them into hands that held everything.
But those two words, they picked me up, they dusted me off, and they gave these stumbling feet direction.
Those two words found me as I was falling, God I was falling, searching, desperate to be a different version of me.

You see,
I grew up loved by most, and clean to some, but found myself hated and dirty to all. The only gift I'd get was glances and glares and the last time I was hugged was, well. . .
Well, people like me don't get hugged.
But those two words changed it all!
They wrapped their arms around me tight, squeezed out death, and offered new life.

Those two words climbed into my ears and broke ground on this abandoned heart. There they made a home. Built a cabin and started a fire to keep those two words warm. Logs have been added daily, nightly, and as those flames grow stronger those two words grow louder. And when He spoke, those two words filled my booth like a cloud of smoke, rushing my mind like waves charging the ocean's shore. Those two words allowed me to drop everything.

And, looking back . . .

I wasn't holding anything.
He saw me far before I had seen Him,
And when I looked up from these hands and into the eyes of this One
Man, value no longer felt like a coin or a scam. He saw me; He looked
right at me, right into me.

Those eyes lit up the atmosphere as He pulled out fear from those in
the vicinity; His eyes held no judgment but stared intently with a vision
of compassion.

When you read it you say it,
But when he spoke it He said it.
He said,
"Follow me!"

Eight letters, five consonants, three vowels, three syllables formed
those two words as they rolled out His mouth.
There wasn't magic in His tone, but perfect grace that cast out doubt,
which set these burdened bones free.

These words weren't a gimmick and didn't leave the mouth of a cynic.
They didn't evaporate into hollow air, but hallelujah! Grace like rain, they
fell on dry ears.
Watering seeds, sprouting roots, spreading like veins pumping hope
through this barely beating heart.
An invitation addressed to me, to leave this life of mine behind.

I felt hope in my knees as I stood to the King taking the first step of
the rest of my life. We walked down that broken road where I once fell.
Heads turned as eyes grew wide, while children whispered questions
that parents let slide.

That long awaited night I walked in the shadow of a crownless King.
I followed next to the one who set me free,
Who set me free from who I used to be.

Those two words broke ground for the cabin whose fireplace burns bright in this heart tonight!
The cabin of my heart is where those two words live, breathe, and there those two words will never die. We add logs to that fire and lift clean hands high and clear eyes to the light in the night sky as I remember the night I died.

And I followed Him all over.
People called me his disciple, but He called us his friends.
People called Him a liar, but we called Him Lord.
We sat seaside and listened to stories that sang like songs,
And we stood on hilltops as He broke bread with the same hands that forgave wrongs.
We watched Him redefine what was possible and what it meant to love.

Man, all He ever wanted to talk about was love.
And He spoke those two words to more than just me,
He spoke those two words to every ear He could find,
Extending an invitation to the lost, broken, and blind.
Each time those two words jumped from his lips they sounded just as sincere as the time they reached out and caught me as I was falling.
And those two words are still spoken to the falling.

And if you're falling,
God I know what it's like to always feel like you're falling,
Let those two words catch you.

God, I swear I'll never be as cold as I was before you came,
and God, I swear I'll never forget the day my life was caught by those two words.

"Follow me" wasn't a plea, it was a cure to a disease.
So if you're falling,
God I know what it's like to be falling–
Let those two words catch you.

....

Those two words are the outstretched hands to catch the falling.

GLORY TO YOU ALONE //

Glory to God alone.
To You the Almighty.
To You, my strength when
I,
well,
I am weak.
To You, the oceans roar like an unending orchestra, never ceasing to
crash a song of freedom casting out fear.
To You, the sun bows to the Son who was sent rising above the rest,
and
I
need
rest.
To You, who holds forever and present time, a watch-full, a watchful
eye.
To You, who has not forgotten since day one, but cannot remember our
sin, meaning what He said when He said it was done.
To You be all the honor and praise, my life in Your hands for the rest of
my days.

Glory to You alone.

HONEST PRAYER //

again
i'm saying
"God, i don't know."

praying

lost and found
below and between
constant confusion

keep me
somewhere between
grace and peace.

YOU //

why am i thinking
so much
about me
when it's about

You?

i remember reading something like
less of me and
more of

You

less of me and more
of

You

less of me and more of

You.

You.

CARRY ME //

i'm saving myself
by shutting it off
turning from noise
toward silence

for good
this goodbye
has no return

it's
walk or remain
carry me
carry through
get me
get through

leave behind what's keeping you alive
only to find you'll survive

carry me
carry through
get me
get through

COME FORWARD //

come forward
there has always been
room

come forward
there is space for you
to hold

a hope
a home
a seat at the table
a place where you
can be you

remove your shoes
stay a while

there is space for you
to hold.

BRAVE //

it is brave
to leave behind
what was meant
to stay in the past

COME TO ME //

dirty hands
and dirty feet
and still
He says
come
to
me

YOUR NAME //

give me what i
need to believe
mercy triumphs
and
grace reigns
and
Love is still
Your name

PAST THE START //

give me a glimpse of more
something i can't ignore
because these two hands
need something to
hand this heart
to remind myself
we are past
the start

TURN ME //

turn me towards
something better
further from myself
and closer to
You

THE //

I don't remember how the last line of this poem goes,
But the end cannot find us if we never begin.

Written from the same hand,
You and I are living stories of a different kind,
Each day offering life to stain a white page,
Breathings from our heart to move beyond the start.
And I've got a little something left to live,
For the ink to dry a line at a time.

I'm folding down the corners of the memories that burned and meant
the most.
Like losing her at the end of chapter two and stumbling upon solace in
the midst of the thunder storms I tried to undo.
I've underlined stories to go back and read,
Crossed out what I can't erase,
Found your polaroid tucked between chapters seven and eight.

It's the words that paint the picture as proof, bringing me back to spring
in the south,
Outside her brick house
Where the wildflowers stretched North,
Blooming without a doubt, like we did at the end of chapter nine.

It's all been written down with swords and pens,
Blood and ink
Reminding us of the narratives of how we used to act and think.

Living, like writing, drives us home,
Leading us down roads of mile marker memories and cable line collections.

We're all a constant work in progress, stuck under construction, slowing
to another detour never planned.

Foot on the gas, it reminds me of the past–
Of what was,
Of who I've become.

I drive to keep from becoming numb,

Like writing, it's how I deal with how I feel.

Pen stained palms,
Hands on the wheel.

I'm checking my rearview mirror once more,
Wondering what it'd be like to rewrite chapters three and four.
If I had made a right where I went left, would I be left feeling like everything
is right?
The quiet things no one knows are trapped in chapter five,
And I've torn out those six senseless pages so many times,
I've got papercut battle scars and new memories on both hands.
But I won't ever forget how good it felt to scribble down chapter ten,
And I can't help but think it wouldn't feel this way if it weren't for way
back when—
Back when I was writing with faded ink from a chewed up pen,
Misspelling with passion, living inside present time, instead of tracing
over what's been.

It's the chapters we can't erase . . . and the ones we want to frame,
The days you tried to keep up and the ones that let you down.
It's the silent moments no one will ever hear,
And the days your lungs shout to disappear.
It's about learning how to come alive when you're bored to death,
And how to write in a comma when you need to catch your breath.

Having written through the rain and fear, it's all becoming more clear.

Living isn't about the last line, but continuing to write the story to the end.

We're all living notes from the past,
Sliding smiles and secrets beneath the surface
Hoping our story will last,
Passing questions and confessions with looks and glances
For our lives to be read again by future writers and poets,
To be known beyond what we understand.
Write it well. Let the ink of each piece dry in peace.
Scribble in grace where the darkness seeks a turn.
Rewrite hope, etch in forgiveness, and

Replace hate with love.

Write it well.
Let the ink dry in peace.

For the end cannot find us if we never begin.

OTHER //

Give it time.
You'll make it to the other side, but for now—
For now—you are here,
Where uncertainty and questions and truth and dad jokes collide and live side by side
Where everything is visible and out of sight;
Wild & calm.
Here, where there aren't enough cups of coffee or smiles or tacos
Where seven billion of us stand together and alone beneath the sun and moon;
Storms and stars

But give it time.

You'll make it to the other side,
And for now . . .

Come alive.

Throw a pizza party.
Order a milkshake, order two milkshakes, order everyone a milkshake.
Get lost within the beauty of daydreaming, only to wake to chase them down.
Listen like every sentence is a secret and it's third grade again, and they are asking, "Do you want to know who likes you?"
Check yes when you can.
Respond with kindness.
Replace hate with love.
Spread hope like Nutella, because we can never have enough of both.

Search for answers with humility,
Live with palms face up,
Give grace to the dark places of your life,
And when you dance,
Because you were made to dance,
Dance like no one's watching
And if they are, give them something to see.

Seek a forever beyond the heavy chaos of living and evening traffic and grocery stores full of hard avocados and broken smiles.

Find magic and don't let it go.
Embrace the weird.
Protect passion.
Meet peace in the escaping present.

And like Grandma said,
"Count your blessings," and when you get to a-million-and-one,
don't be done—start again.

Hold on to compassion and curiosity as you step and stumble to
where you are going.
And when you stumble get up and keep going.

Keep going like it's going to be okay.
Face fear.
Pray on bent and broken knee
Stand up and step again
And when you stand to step
Step to stand up for what is right
Stand up against what is wrong
Stand up for those who have gone on
Pause in the presence of beauty and photograph the memory with
your own.

Risk everything even if you're the only one who sees why
Chase a sunset and take a bite out of the cotton candy sky
Stay for tomorrow,
Live with more love than yesterday
Walk with the weary
And learn their songs and sing them with your soul

Write and speak honest words of love
Shout a song of celebration and
Celebrate good news.

Scream beneath the rain until your mouth fills with a sip and let that
sip turn into a smile.

Create art and nachos and sandcastles and share them with our world.
Tell your story, the one you're living, the one that is changing our world,
because you are changing our world.
And watch.

Watch it continue to spin and change.

Invite others to join the change
Take root and hold each other up
Call patience close and push comparison far, far away
And be the awakened.
Remain the awakened.

Go North to South, East to West
Sit on a front porch and be.
Just be.
Be present.

Give it time
and we will get to the other side.

I'M TRYING //

I'm trying.

Sometimes it's all I have to say.

I'm trying.

I'm tempted to think these two words are a cop out
or an excuse, a cry from the weak.
But sometimes life is heavy
and hard
and all the things we don't want it to be.

And these are the words that are left:

I'm trying.

They've become exhausted
and are exhausting to say.
I'm trying.

Out of breath.
You're okay.
Inhale.
Go on.
Exhale.
Keep going.
Deep breath.
You're not done yet.
I'm trying.

And sometimes that's all we can say.
And I want to believe these two words are enough;
to believe I am enough.

And I know these two words aren't the end even when
I feel far away from today.
I'm trying.

Out of breath.

You're okay.

Inhale.

Go on.

Exhale.

Keep going.

Deep breath.

You're not done yet.

SOME DAYS //

Some days you'll need the open road and loud nostalgic music.
You'll need phone calls with family and conversations with old friends.
Some days you'll need the rain and you'll need the window down.
Some days you'll need to get out of the car and take a picture in the
middle of the road, or pull over to watch the sunset.
Most days you'll need a cup of coffee and an open Bible.
And you'll need to get a refill on both.

Some days you just need to be reminded that today is another day.
And you'll need to do things to remind yourself that you're you and
you're alive to live.

But everyday we will need each other and we will need to be reminded
that we aren't alone.
Everyday we will need meaningful hugs and hopeful smiles.
We will need to hear we are loved and that it's ok for us to be ourselves.
Some days we will have to ask to be told these things; other days honest
words of love will be freely spoken into our lives.

And those are the days we live for.

Those are the days that keep us alive.

And being alive is a good thing.

This poem was inspired by Jamie Tworkowski,
founder of To Write Love On Her Arms.

TREES //

All things grow from something.

Like you and I.
My memories lay full like the forest we call home.
We sprouted from a single seed, raised to grow up among the trees.
We grew in our grave knowing our roots kept us
home in our place.
Nurtured with words, we kicked the dirt, were welcomed with a whisper
of a warm wind as we floated through the fog to kiss the clouds.
We lived in the shadows of the undersides of their leaves, and every
night before the sky closed its eye, we reached for the dimming light.

Day by day,
Side by side,
you and I.

Words watered our life, keeping our veins full,
coursing them with what we need to reach our home.
We bathed in drops, struggled in droughts; downpours were a holiday,
but it was the morning mist that meant the most.

And in the morning, it was still you and I.
It's always been you and I.
In the shadow of one another we grew North.
Late one May you got ahead of me, but June I hit a spurt and saw your
peak grow into me, like the sun setting into the sea.

Summer and Spring brought warmth,
Fall strangled us, giving us Joseph's coat
that was stripped off our arms before we needed it the most.
The cold kept us close,
but no matter the temperature we burned with hope.
And I'll reach for you as you reach for me,
hide our roots like hands under sheets.
No one can see,
but everyone knows you're holding me and I'm holding you.

As we began to stretch for the sky's eye our limbs were climbed by the
arms of mankind

They gave you a swing set and me a house,
made from another of our kind.
Piercing our skin like the silver in their ears, they fashioned fun.

Their tiny limbs climbed us, treated us like we were one of them,
hugged us tight as they pulled themselves to our tops. Locking in
laughter, we blew in the wind when they tickled our bark.

We gave them air, but they gave us purpose.

At night they gathered around our chopped friends, burning them bright
and we breathed them in. The smoke clogged our lungs, while their
laughter and stories broke our sadness with joy.

And I wish so badly when we were placed beneath the fold of the earth,
they would have dropped us closer together. As we'd be watered, we'd
twist our roots together, growing towards the heavens, watching the
bellies of God's winged creation float above through the cut out blue
we reached to kiss with our green peaks.

As we reached to the sun, I grew into you as you grew into me.
And I can never be close enough to you,
never can I hold you close enough.
Even when we're full and our arms lock like the hands of man,
you felt so far.

And they cut us down before we could reach the wind.
Our torsos ripped through,
but they couldn't hear our screams over their machines.
I whispered for you to stay strong, they'll place us where we belong,
but never grow weary of being strong.
They must have seen something in us to desire us.
We feared this was our story coming to a close,
our last chapter being written by the hands of man.
Like Romeo and Juliet, the tale we heard told as the child read aloud
with her back placed to your feet.
Tragedy met romance, but romance triumphs devastation.
And the sun must have been shining bright as they kept us
side by side,

Like I said,

Day by day,
side by side,
You and I.

I'll always be by your side.

And they shipped us on flat tops, we passed fields of those still stand-
ing, waiting for their time to endure the silver pain of the blade.
They laid us on a hill. We thought this is where it would all come to a
close, but we found hope in a renewed life.

And one piece of me, one piece of you at a time, they placed us closer
together, intertwining our insides, mixing together our outsides. Silver
splinters sparked us together, nailing us on top of each other.

I couldn't even guess which part of me is me and which part of you is you.

....

We now stand as walls and a roof.
We grew together to create a home, a symbol of hope.
Together we keep out the dark,
we keep out the snow for two seeds to stay warm and close.

And
I wouldn't want to be built into a home with anyone else but you.
I wouldn't want to be anywhere with anyone else but you.
Home is found in another, and I found a home in you.

Day by day,
Side by side,
You and I.

GIVE AND TAKE //

give and take
but not without
a little ache
to go with
a lot of constant
wonder
of
then
and
now
and
forever

GROUND //

do you feel the
rebellion rising within
there's a fight in my heart
a war waged in my hands
a breaking rope
tied
to an anchored soul
this hope i know
it is
falling
floating
fleeing
do you feel
these sinking feet
seeking solid ground
now
will you
move these eyes toward
holy ground

LETTER //

I've been writing inside, beneath snow covered pines, shivering through the day and drowning in a sea of blankets by night; feeding on questions, wrestling with fear and pride, drinking black coffee in the morning and writing in a black notebook with the moon in sight.
It's been a couple years, but I'm still here.
I've spent seasons alone, something no man should ever do.
I made my home on a couch, and gave up among its cushions.
With still hands I've been tempted to taste the sweet temptation to forget all that I've become and
start living like someone I didn't want to be.
Inside I stood between four walls of confusion born out of boredom and television.
Alone was redefined by silence and solitude.

But with you I felt alive to be me.

To ask questions and sit with uncertainty like it's ok.
To be the man who knows he's got much to learn and see.
To run like a kid, wild and free, like every day is
Saturday and sunny.
To adventure in my favorite pair of pants
and with dirt under my fingernails.

To live uncomfortable and hopeful,
because there isn't any other way to live.

But I've started comparing again, this and that,
thinking I'm not good enough.
Like I'm caught between being the man I never thought I'd be and the man I want to become.
I've witnessed with both lungs that comparison collapses the joy found within freedom.
And freedom is addressed to us inviting us to scream under the rain, to remind ourselves we are okay.

We're okay.

I guess this is just another letter to me for you to read.
And I'd rather let you come inside than leave you outside.

I'd rather live with these questions
than live trying to be my own answer.
And I'd rather go together than alone.
Since we last hit record, I've come a long way.
Distance can't be measured with money or fame,
but with hope and grace.
With the way I stand to each day, the look on your face.
The space between the man and the mirror
and the life inside these bones.
Let's never lose our sense of wonder, or ourselves to stagnancy.
Let out dreams not become past desires or ideas that once looked
good when the light hit them right, but let's fly with them through the
day and night.
Let courage and mercy be found in our words and with hope may we
contribute to the greater good.
With all things in his hands,
Let's nudge one another towards life,
to live alive full of joy and insight.
Never allowing fear to tie itself around our wrists,
or trample our mind
Never hide behind a lie or keep the inside from seeing the outside.
Let's write, speak, and live honest words of love.
Let's open up our hearts and invite others inside.

Dear you,

This is just another letter to me
for you to read.

SORROW //

i see you,
sorrow.

stay awhile.

but,

not too long.

i've got to move on.

ONWARD //

i'm yelling
"onward"
and maybe one day i'll
hear myself
and leave this mess
i've made
behind
and maybe one day i'll
join hands with
grace
and never look back behind
and maybe one day i'll
face my fears and place them inside
the palms of peace
leaving them back behind
because one day i'll be leaving this all back behind
i'll leave you
moving onward
whispering
for you
to do the same

do the same
yell
"onward"
and listen
and yell it again if you need
feel the freedom found
in this one word
onward.

we're yelling
"onward."

WORTHY //

you're clearing the confusion
of this one-sided conversation
a slow and hold steady reminder
that you're still speaking

Worthy

EMPTY MORNING //

Every morning my thoughts flow free, rushing wildly without a hint, a drop of grace.

My eyes fall downcast to the floor; my step sluggishly walks. My shoulders support the weight of my past, slung over my shoulder, whispering negativity as the day slows by.

And these hands juggle my faults, fractures, and failures, leaving me stiff and sore.

Like all of my bones dried up overnight, empty of love, replaced with shame, like a river caught in a drought; aching for a glimmer of hope, a drop of rain.

Life lives somewhere in these bones, I know it does, but where I can't find, and I've sought to search to seek, but have been left empty handed, full of my own baggage.

I want so badly to come alive; to pump hope up and down, in and out of my life.

I want, like a tree, like the one in Psalm 1, to reflect hope and strength.

To catch the sun breaking free though the branches of the trees that sprouted from a seed by the waters of life.

I want to stand with roots stretched deep, grasping, reaching through the dirt underneath, keeping firm through the storms that pour.

But I feel like the furthest thing from the tree, the furthest thing from me.

Well, what am I, well, I don't know. I'm full of questions and wonder do all of us struggle with identity? Do all of us struggle with what we were, with what we went through, with what we would never wish on anybody?

There are some things we can't get back.

Things we didn't know had value. We priced them as nothing, and now we tell everyone who will listen that they are everything, for we gave them away for nothing.

And when you give everything away for nothing, you are left feeling like nothing.

I've trusted my heart, only to be left lost and crushed. You'd think I'd come to believe it is deceitful like Jeremiah says, but I've gone and trusted the heart I was told to guard.

I never thought a simple decision could have such repercussions or could scar the way they have.

And I know Jesus, I know you forgive and you've forgiven, but even if you've forgotten my stain, I can't scrub it clean from the surface of my brain.

And this isn't me lacking faith, or is it? Because, Jesus, I know what you've done, what you did. I know how you love, because every time we sing "How He Loves", chills run up and down, and up and down my spine causing tears to flow from these eyes, and they flow so freely as if they desire to fill the dried up river, where the tree I dream to be begins to sprout from a seed.

I don't know—maybe this is just another sad poem, or maybe this is honesty at its finest.

And we're only as free as we want to be, but to be free we have to believe.
I sing, we've sang about our chains being broken, but I'm still shackled to the sins he's shaken.

I'm holding onto what he's let go, so where's the faith in that?
I'm caught with both hands on decisions made that I can't take back, that I can't change.

Like, I can't forget the way I let you in, the way you ripped me limb from limb.
I can't change the actions of my eyes or hands
and I can't take back the words I should have never said.

I can't erase the thoughts from the way it was when it was the way it was, the way it should have never been.

But I know, like the tree in Psalm 1 there is hope,
there is growth for those who plant themselves by the river flow,
who walk in the way of righteousness.
Down under the waves in the grains of sand rests a glimpse of the Last Day when everything circulating this clogged mind is forever washed away, and the river rushes free with an abundant, overflowing amount of peace.

AREN'T WE ALL //

aren't we all
walking destinations
traveling different directions
crossed paths and crooked lines
mixed dirt
broken rhymes
stumbled stories
crumpled maps
wrong ways gone right
and right ways gone wrong
aren't we all
searching
to belong
searching
for
home
and don't we know
we are
another's
home
walking destinations

I'VE BEEN TRYING //

i've been trying

and maybe i should leave it there

i've been trying to forget

to unclench white knuckled fists
to see it from where you sit
to make sense of why
to drop my pointed finger
to rest in praying hands
to let empathy empty
and forgiveness fill

but i'm still shaken from being still

i've been trying

and maybe i should leave it there

i've been trying

i'll continue in this echo

as i empty
as you fill.

I'M WAITING //

i'm waiting for you to stare right through me
beyond what i hold up for you to see
convincing you of who i've come to be
but i'm caught cold between clear and cloudy
in this circus i've created
acting as a human doing
rather than living as a human being
a human hiding
on stage
in the shadows of the spotlight
so you'll always and only see
part of me

living inside the darkness
caught cast in a dim light
offering prideful care from stage left
bringing forward a manicured script
so you'll think nothing is wrong
and
i
am
always
right.

A HARD TIME //

"I'm just giving you a hard time."

Oh, okay.

The last thing I need is a hard time.
If you want to give me something
pour me some wine
and tell me I'm doing just fine.
Bake me a cupcake.
Really, any kind of gluten will do.
Croissants, cinnamon rolls, donuts.
Compliment my pants for goodness sake
or
For crying out loud
or
For pete's sake.
I mean, for my sake.

Stop giving me a hard time.

I have a hard time understanding why
we have to give each other a
hard time?
"A hard time"
I've never wanted a
hard time.
It's never been on my
Christmas list.
Neither has underwear.
But I still get that, too.
But I need underwear.
I don't need a hard time.
Give me a smile.
Tell me a joke.
A knock-knock joke.
A joke that will send a tear down my cheek.
One where laughter will steal my breath.
But not a hard time.
That will only keep me down.

Play me a song.
Write me a poem.
Give me queso or guacamole.
Something I can dip a chip in.
I can't dip a chip in a hard time.

I've checked the calendar and there is no time for a hard time.
There is coffee time.
and nap time.
and party time
but I do not have time for you to give me a
hard time.

WILD //

it is wild
but it is well
center me still
to be
as You
will

TAKE AWAY //

will you take away
what's been taking me away

will you keep me from
what's been keeping me from

will you replace what's been
taking up time and space

TAKE ME //

take me a bit beyond myself
to see where
i've been
to be where
you are
take me a bit beyond myself
to see it's You
who has taken me this far

SHAME //

i'm done letting
shame
hold space
here i stand
revived
by grace
fighting to remain
in the life
He's changed

SIDE //

I desire to write new words down; to see something that flows
left to right across this smudged screen.
I'm trying to get past writer's block, but find myself running straight into
brick wall after brick wall after brick wall.
I'm looking for a door to walk through; to escape where I am; to step
out of the storm.
I want to clutch the doorknob, twist, and push my way through to the
promised land other side, but this brick wall doesn't have a door.

Or a window.

I feel enclosed, blind to the outside—stuck alone on the inside.
Hope seems far, while weariness and frustration grow quick like weeds.
Maybe I should close my computer and walk away.
Or sit on the couch within eyesight and read a book.
Or watch Back To The Future II on Netflix.

But I think I'll save that for tonight.

Coffee always helps,
But these teeth are moving further from ideal pearly whites.

Giving up isn't an option.
I'll get past this brick wall, I'll make it to the other side.
Maybe I'll grab a ladder or a shovel

But I want to work to get to the other side.

I want the hammer.
A big hammer.
A hammer that needs two hands.
Not Thor's, but my own.
Rage and frustration will propel me to pound straight into the brick wall.
Vibrations will shake these arms, but I will not be stopped.

I will chip, crack, and break that wall,
but I will not chip, crack, or break at all.

Shock will meet sweat, but I will not stop.

I'll shatter the bricks to see through to the other side.
I'll close my eyes and grit my teeth and wipe my brow.
I'll grip tight and rip my skin and I won't get woozy when the blood mixes with the dirt.
I'll curse and spit and ask for forgiveness and repeat.
I'll ignore the lies inside my mind that tell me to go lay down inside.
I'll wave off the pain in my back.
I'm moving forward.
The wrinkles are growing deep around my eyes with every hit, every wince.

And maybe I should give up.

Maybe I should have just climbed the wall.

And maybe the hammer isn't my tool of choice.

It isn't.

I prefer the spork.

You know,
the spoon shaped utensil with tines at the tip to scoop and stab.

But I will not give up.

I will knock this brick wall down.
I will see the other side.
And I will write something that matters.
The screen will hold new words and
These words will act like a hammer in these calloused hands.
These words will tear down the brick walls within the mind of the writer and reader.
I will write something that someone, somewhere can relate to.
Someone.
Somewhere.

And somewhere someone will see this isn't about writer's block.
Somewhere someone will nod their head and see through the brick wall.

They'll see this brick wall isn't really a brick wall, but it is fear.
It is uncertainty.
It is depression.
It is the questions that swarm.
It is wondering if I am taking steps in the right direction or if I am just taking steps.
It is a crossroads, a tossing and turning all night, an unshakeable thought.
It is regret and anxiety and waking to another Monday that should be Saturday or at the earliest Sunday.
It is the constant battle between love and pain and I'm growing weary from fighting.
They'll see the hammer as tears.

Or confession.
Or prayer.
Or another cup of coffee.
Or an honest conversation.
Or a hug that lasts too long, but not long enough.
They'll see through the line about a spork as a poor attempt to distract from speaking openly.
From saying what needs to be said.
The shifting of the rudder to steer the conversation off course so you'll stop looking at me as a crazy person.
I'm not a crazy person.

And they'll know this wasn't about writer's block.

But this is about living.

This is about continuing.

This is about waking up and saying okay.
Saying I'm okay.
Saying we're okay.
Saying it's going to be okay.
Even when there is a brick wall.
Even when it's Monday.
Even when fear,
And depression,
And regret
Tell you it isn't going to be okay,
It will be okay.
Every day.
I'm okay.
We're okay.

It's going to be okay.

Welcome to the other side.

CREATE //

i can't see through the soil
but i don't need to see
to believe
something is happening

beneath and below

sometimes we don't see
the creation
but something is being
created

lodged deep like a seed
beneath and below

beneath and below
beginning to grow.

SORRY //

i'm sorry
you never got to see
the me
who left before i knew
how to be me

but because of you

i am who

i've become

MOUNTAIN //

The end appears different from the beginning.

Like the tree and the seed; the boy and the man.
It's something I can't shake, something I've tried to leave behind, but something that continues to chase as I close my eyes.

My thoughts run faster than my mouth and my jaw falls with the weight of the world pushing upon my shoulders. A mind circling and juggling what ifs, attempting to bury a past with hands that still feel broken and dirty despite the bread and wine; despite spoken words of life.

They say my faith isn't strong enough or I don't believe enough, but I know anxiety has eight legs and it crawls, casting webs, clouding up time, filling space inside the darkness of mind.
They don't know enough to say I don't believe enough,
because I believe when Christ walked, lived, and died He rose for those thorns in my side.

Those thorns love the darkness, like anxiousness loves loneliness.

There in the shadows they fire fracturing fears aiming at my faith, and faith is something you either have or don't.
And God believe me, I do.
The scars on my knees, like the scar on His side, remind me how I've called His name day and night, and day and night I believe God is working, changing me by the boldness of His grace.

My doubts could move mountains, but the beauty of doubting is that it can lead to faith,
and faith pushes the mountain farther from where it was placed.

We meet fear with faith, and let our faith displace fear.

My life changed when the pen stroked across the page sculpting an idea, one still hard to believe, but one that pumps life back in our failing lungs.

Your mountain is not meaningless.

It's not.

Your mountain does not define you or describe you.
Your mountain is an invitation to climb.
And mountains were not created to be climbed alone
and you were not created to climb alone.

In times of desperation we aim for restoration.

We step as children of the light, dispelling the darkness together one step at a time, one step at a time we close the space between here and there, climbing closer to home.
We step to bring the light to the darkness, stretching ourselves closer to love, hope, and security.
In all that is heavy we seek the light, we keep the fight.
We build with love, and love never ends.

Our end doesn't have to look like the beginning.

SPEAK UP | LISTEN UP //

Speak up.

Speak up like everyone is listening, even if no one is near.
Speak up like you just conquered your biggest fear.
Speak up with your hands, move them side to side, up and down, create shadow puppets, tell a story of a man who wanted to speak up and learned to do so without his mouth.
Speak up with nickels, pennies, and dimes spend them on the poorest kids in town.
Speak up, step into your words, the ones you've been shouting for years on the inside and are finally ready for them to see the outside.
Speak up like those words have been building since the day you were born and you're about to give birth to the first honest sentence you've ever formed.
Speak up like your lungs are full of love and you've been asked to fill the world with one word at a time.
Speak up like you just met Jesus and He was walking with your grand-father and both of their arms wrap around you tight.
Speak up like tonight is the last night, or the first night, but regardless it's a night, and you're alive so, speak up!
Speak up for you can assume that the one in front of you is going through something you wouldn't wish on your worst enemy.
Speak up like you were meant to live for more than what you've been living for and you realized there is such a thing as a fresh beginning.
Speak up like you just won free chips and guacamole for the rest of your life.

Speak up.

Speak up for the sensitive, the sarcastic, and the stubborn.
Speak up for the segregated, the separated, and the sophisticated.
Speak up for the weak, the lost, the silent, the silenced.
Speak up for the forgotten.
Speak up for the fallen.
Speak up for the fathers who can't speak to their daughters.
Speak up for the sons who grew up without a mother.
Speak up for those who can't find the words to tell their story and think their life lacks glory.

Speak up.

Speak up like your future wife just caught your eye for the very first time and you can't help but say something.

Say something.

Speak up.

Speak up and ask her name, her favorite color.
Be bold.
Ask her to the doo-wop, tell her you love her, propose with a ring-pop, drive all night, take a coffee pit stop, propose again, whisper sweet nothings, and then yell it from a mountain top.
Speak up on bent knee, stand to your feet and say it again and don't stop saying it because we should not stop saying, "I love you."

I love you.

Which is why I am speaking up.

And then listen up.

Because sometimes we need to stop speaking up so we can listen up.
To close our mouths and let our ears capture the light in all that is heavy.
To hold our tongues and wait in silence for another to speak up, because every teacher has been a student, and even teachers are students, and for us to learn we need to seek the silence.

So, listen up.

Listen up, log off, power down, sit back with ears anticipating words of hope and direction.
Listen up with eyes wide and palms face up.
Listen up like listening is the latest hipster fad.
Listen up like she said your name and it sent guilty chills up and down your spine because you did something bad.
Listen up like you're in the front row of Shakespeare's last show or maybe you're being told how to escape because you can't stand

Shakespeare with all his doths, 'tis, thous, and those confusing monologue vows.

Listen up like the words circling the air are a rare occurrence, a breath of fresh air.

Listen up for you can assume the one in front of you is going through something you wouldn't wish on your worst enemy.

Listen up like your best friend said, "Tonight is the night and I need you to proofread the suicide note I wrote."

Listen up like your son came to you and said, "Dad, I made a mistake, and I, I just don't know."

Listen up like you woke to a cold sweat and prayed to God to pull the deepest regrets from the furthest cavity of your aching chest.

Listen up like you heard about a Man who says,
"Come to me all who are weary and I will give you rest."

Listen up like you just heard about forgiveness and someone said something about it being for you.

Listen up like Santa Claus and the Easter Bunny just walked in the room and said, "We know a thing or two about you."

Listen up like the barista yelled your name and your mochaccino-frappe-with-an-extra-pump-of-doesn't-taste-like-coffee is up.

Listen up because someone might be explaining belly buttons and how lint gets in them.

Listen up like she said, "We need to talk."

Listen up like you just got done shedding your last tear and now you're ready to hear.

Listen up like you're willing to bet the best hasn't happened yet.

Listen up like life is beginning to climb, heading for the up and up.

Listen up like the sun is rising to shine and shame is no longer the center of your life.

Listen up like you finally decided to live until you die, instead of living to one day die.

Listen up like the first time she walked by and for a beautiful second your heart and time seemed to stop.

Listen up like when you finally mustered the courage and asked her her name and you stood in silence waiting for what she'd say.

Listen.

Listen up like when she said, "I love you."

Listen up, take it in, with ears open, judgments abandoned, and hands ready to begin.
Listen up to understand, to hear the words of heartache flowing from fear and failure.
Listen up, pull back what's being spoken, dive inside, feel the words, the rhythm, the rhyme.
Listen up, stretch out your hand to catch the words being said, put them in your pockets, lay them out on your bed, hold them tight, share them with a friend.

And listen up.

Listen up to realize words reach just like hands and can do as much good as they can bad.
Listen up like every spoken word is an earth-shattering headline and you're holding the paper in your hands.

Listen up, for someone might say something that will change your life and . . .

They might ask you to speak up.

FOR US //

Jesus,
You didn't fight back.
Not even when You had the chance.
You stood still.
A stamp of betrayal on Your cheek ignited the events for the coming week.
But Jesus, You didn't run,
You didn't budge and
above all You didn't even hold a grudge.
Your words knocked them to the ground.
Laid out;
Face down.
Confused and un-amused they had not a word to say as they hauled
You away.
Broken and bound by their chains Your heart didn't change, it stayed
the same,
pumping blood to Your veins, so You could endure the world's pain.
Cracking Your head; whipping Your back for answers to questions
they asked.
When You spoke the truth they asked for ears turned only to ignore.

No crown for a king,
Just a thick bouquet of thorns to cut and sting.
They pulled out words of axes and began to cut You down;
Stomping their fellow man into the ground.
With tongues like camels they spit on You relentlessly and with a strong
sense of intensity.

But Jesus,
You didn't fight back.
Not even when You had the chance,
You stood still.
And when they ripped and stripped Your blood soaked, band-aid
acting cloak You didn't give in to give up, You never muttered or uttered
"Enough!" no matter how rough and tough were the big, the bad, and
the buff.
They handed You a cross and with a whip in hand they demanded,
"Walk."

A trail laced with tears they watched in shock.

Poisonous slurs;
Demeaning words
Creep into the mind of He who faces death.
Crowds the size of stadiums came to witness You tread the blood-stained dirt road in hopes to catch a glance of Your last breath.
But Jesus,
You didn't fight back.
Not even when You had the chance.
You stood still.

And You had the chance!
But You stood still,
You stood still for the world,
for the ones You love,
for Your children,
for me,
for us!

And when Your robe was torn off and when the nails went in—You flinched—of course You flinched.
You were human.

You once
Ate, laughed, and cried.
You once walked, talked, and taught.
You healed and revealed.
You prayed and forgave.
You, like the storm, were still!
While hanging on the cross You could have gotten down,
Of course You could have gotten down.
You're God.
But You didn't.
Hanging there, hardly able to breathe, speak, see, You prayed.
You prayed for those who hated You.
You prayed for those who took Your words, your hands, Your heart and twisted, beat, and broke them.

But You did not fight back.
You didn't.

You endured the sin of the world—our sin—my sin.
On Your back it weighed You down like a sack packed full of our dirt,
our shame, our lies, our hate, our disgrace
but You hung there high, while the others cried, You yelled to the sky,
belting it out from Your insides, shattering the earth only for people to
run and hide, and now, and now no longer were you disguised.

Our sin drowned You for three whole days.
Laid to rest,
laid to waste only to come back and give us a new taste of what it
means to never forsake.
The ground it could not bound the love of the Son.
It could not contain the once beaten, broken, breathless One.

Jesus,
You didn't fight back.
Not even when You had the chance.
You stood still.
For us You didn't fight back.
For us You stood still.

UP & OUT //

from the ground up
and out
like there is a magnet somewhere up
and out
in the clouds
and somehow i remain
somewhere in my head
trying to get up
and out

TODAY, I AM A WRITER //

Left boot first.
Right boot second.
You can't go to work without your work boots.
I fill up a bottle of water and a cup of coffee.
Both filtered.
My mind still cloudy, but it's beginning to clear.
I grab my keys and clip them on my belt loop.
Back right.
Not one of the front loops.
I'm not a dad at a theme park.
I have my standards.
I check my backpack and make sure I have all I need.
Computer. Notebook. Charger. Pen. Another pen. My favorite pen. My
backup pen. Headphones. Sunglasses. Calendar.
I put my hat on.
It doesn't fit right. I haven't found a hat that fits well.
Sometimes I feel like the hat.
I just don't fit.
My head is small and sometimes I wonder if that's why I forget to finish
my sentenc
I leave the house and lock the blue door behind me.
Unlock my car as I get closer.
The headlights blink and I wonder if I have enough pens.
I do my phone, keys, wallet dance.
I pat my front right pocket and hit my phone.
I shake my keys like I am the world's best tambourine player.
Maybe I am.
I touch my back pocket and only feel my back pocket.
No wallet.
Lock my car.
Turn around.
I always forget my wallet.
I fold it open, checking for money.
Nothing.
I am a writer.
Today, I am a writer.
I drive to a coffee shop while listening to a podcast.
Something about being creative.
Something that will inspire me to write the world's greatest book or

poem or tweet.

Watch out Shakespeare.

I walk inside the coffee shop with my backpack on and smile at the baristas.

We are on a first name basis.

Hudson. PJ. Taylor. Marco. Michael.

They know I'll eventually buy a coffee from them, but right now, I've "got a lot of work to do" because it's another "busy season".

I sit down in the corner, my favorite spot.

A plug for my computer is near.

I try to concentrate, but I need coffee.

I walk back to the counter and they already know my order.

Black coffee.

Back to work.

I sit down and place my computer in front of me.

Coffee to the right.

Water to the left.

Phone on the table.

Upside down. I will not be distracted today.

Sip.

Look up.

No one recognizes me as the guy whose pre-scheduled tweet got 1 retweet and 3 favorites and I wonder why.

I know why.

No one approaches me to ask if I'm the guy who wrote that one blog post about that one current event that is no longer relevant.

Get over yourself.

Meet and greet is over.

It's time to write.

I don't connect to the internet.

Today I am a writer.

And today I will write.

Focus.

Write. Focus. Write. Focus. Write. Focus.

Write.

Blink.

Distraction.

I should probably check to see if I have any new followers.

Maybe that scheduled tweet took off.

Turn internet on.

But only for a minute.

Facebook. Nothing. Scroll. Like. Comment. Share. Scroll. Compare.

Close out.

Twitter. Nothing. Scroll. Favorite. Retweet. Compare.

Close out.

Instagram. Nothing. Double tap. Scroll. Double tap. Scroll. Compare.

Close out.

Find an inspiring blog post by a professional writer.

He tells me I should be making money for my work.

I still don't.

That's not why I do this, but it gives me something to mention in this line.

This line, too (see the line above).

Time keeps passing and the day is slipping away.

How has it been 30 minutes?

Am I even a writer?

Doubt creeps.

Doubt yells.

Write.

I've been here for an hour already and only written this much?

Write.

Fight.

Will anyone even read this?

Write.

Bathroom break.

I just want a cinnamon roll.

No, no.

Gluten weighs you down and you don't have money for new pants.

Write.

Focus.

Write.

Twitter.

Close out.

Write.

Does this really matter?

I hate everything. This makes no sense. I make no sense.

Instagram.

Seriously? Just write.

Write.

Focus.
Write.
Sneeze.
Ew.
Sip.
Facebook.
Only one notification? Oh, it's from her, again.
E-mail.
Bathroom break.
LinkedIn. Just kidding.
Focus.
Write.
Sip.
Focus.
Write.
Focus.
Write.
More coffee.
Jitters.
Yikes.
Bathroom.
Write.
Bathroom.
Write.
Go home.

Today, I am a writer.

IT TAKES ONE //

all it took was for one
to speak up
shouting from their depths
whispering what's clutched close
for me to
see myself
to see i am not
have not
and will not be
alone.
and now
i
speak up.

KEEP GOING //

Keep going.
When you don't want to wake up, keep going.
When you wake up and don't want to get out of bed, keep going.
When every step feels like a mountain, keep going.
When you don't want to admit that this is hard, keep going.
When you shudder at the thought of someone finding out, keep going.
When the lies get loud, keep going.
When the lies get even louder, keep going.
When you feel like no one is listening when you begin speaking, keep going.
When you feel like the world would be better without you, keep going.
When you don't want tomorrow to come, keep going.
When the past is hard to swallow, keep going.
When the future freaks you out, keep going.
When nothing seems to be going your way, keep going.
When all you want is for today to be your last day, keep going.
When you can't fall asleep because your thoughts are louder than bombs, keep going.
And when you don't want to do another day again, keep going.
Keep going.
Write it on your hand.
Place it in your heart.
Keep going.

Keep going because we need you to; we want you to.

Keep going because I need you to.

Keep going because some days I don't want to keep going,
but I need you to keep going so I can keep going.

We keep going together.

And we are going somewhere.

We are going somewhere better together.

And we keep going because we are together for each other.

Keep going.

NOTHING WITHOUT SOMETHING //

there is no masterpiece
without a mess
no journey
without steps back
look through the broken and the breaking
to see the beauty
and
it's all worth fighting for

FORGIVEN NOT FORGOTTEN //

most days it's all in my head
lies reaching down to my heart and hands
it's
this
swirling surrounding
and it's pounding
with questions and memories
reminding me of who
and where I've been
and tonight
lead these
knees to the floor
with faith to ask for
grace and peace

to forget what you've forgiven
to surrender what you've forgotten
to silent the swirling surrounding and pounding
within
to believe i've been forgiven
and
not
forgotten.

STILL ME SLOW //

still me slow
to remember the truth i know
that when i speak
You hear.

still me slow
to see the prayer
i've prayed below and above and between
answered

still me slow
to trust
the words you spoke

still me slow
to take
your outstretched hand
and go.

still me slow.

DON'T ERASE THE MAGIC //

don't erase the magic
with perfectionism
or overthinking
i'm so good at overthinking
don't erase the magic
let it be
continue to wander with and within wonder
look around
because this is all for
now
you're here
don't erase the magic

LEAD //

lead my heart to
wonder and wander
in the depths
of where we are going
of where you have already been
to walk with you
through the
now
and
then

HE IS //

something in me
believes
He is
doing more

in me

and with me

and for me

than meets these eyes

BACK OF MY MIND //

in the back of my mind
i continue to find
moments and memories
reminders and realizations
that a little courage
is more than enough

FOUR WORDS //

it's hard to move beyond
what you left behind
but forward is four words:
you are not alone.

NOT DONE //

i hold pain and joy
together
like two colors
blending
becoming one
a waking wonder
a mixed marvel
a reminder
i am not done

I'LL HOPE //

and still
i'll hope
despite the
unknown

i'll hope.

CONTINUE //

continue to seek
continue to listen
continue to trust
continue to serve
continue hope
and above all
continue to love

DEAR YOU, //

I wrote this for you.
An unfinished, never-finished poem played like a symphony from my soul.
Note after note, written, scribbled, rewritten and rescribbled.
These words were written to speak.
To stretch like humbled hands to the lost, broken, and the weak.
Gather round, stand or take a seat.

Dear you,
You in the front to you in the back, and all the hearts that fill the vacant cracks.
To the couple cuddled close and their third-wheel driver.
To the lonely wall clinger and New York City cab rider
To the daughter who can't come to acceptance with her genetics
and spends hours hiding under applied cosmetics.

This is written for you.

To the suit-wearers and briefcase-carriers
and to the homeless men they pass each day.
To the guilt-stained mind who forgot about new mercies found in the sunrise
To the lost teaching that H-O-P-E
comes hand in hand with L-O-V-E
and it's been on sale for F-R-E-E.
To the soaked-shoe school boy walking the wet Portland streets
To the beautiful, bright redhead whose only been known as, "that redhead."
and to the single mother raising three kids while juggling her six part
time jobs on her ten tired fingers,
This is written for you.
To the confused geek and sensitive jock
To the lost cheerleader and new-found believer
To you who reads far into every negative word spoken in your direction;
The twisted words from the twisted tongues that sting and question,
Leaving your answer to be a sniffle and shrug.

This is written for you.

To the 10-year-old buried deep in your soul
And to the dirt you've been meaning to shovel.
To the awkward ages and unhealthy stages,

To the couch potato and those who used to eat play dough.
To the daytime dreamer and your imaginary friend
And to the one-sided talks, and single late-night walks you'll take with him.
This is written for the broken-hearted heroine and her heartbreaker.
To the middle school midget stretching for another inch, and the unappreciated player stuck playing left bench,
To the braceface, four-eyed, five-foot-three fourth grade gal who will one day be crowned homecoming queen.

This is written for you.

To the adopted child with a million questions all beginning with 'why'
And to the parents prayerfully searching for a million answers with teary eyes.
To the midnight snacker and early morning riser.
To the coffee addicts and our coffee breath
To the fairytale dreamer and the Krispy Kreme eater
To the Justin Bieber believers and Michael Jackson mourners

....

This is written for you.

To the absent, alone, and aggravated
To the burnt, bruised, and bent
To the corrupt, crushed, and cured

Here is your invite to come alive every night; to live for more than what meets the eye.
To have new life in this life that will one day be raised with eternal life.
To finally be able to breathe fresh air and not be congested with fear.
And to break the past with forgiveness, and enter the future with eyes clear.

This is written for you.
This is written to speak.
This is written to spark.
This is written for more than the heart,
but for the One who created it to start.

ABOUT THE AUTHOR //

Tanner Olson is a writer, storyteller, and the creator of Written to Speak, a spoken word and writing project that seeks to share hope and announce love. Tanner currently serves at ACTS Church Lakeline in Austin, Texas as their Director of Community and Communications. He loves breakfast food, Orlando Magic basketball, dogs, coffee, and his wife, Sarah.

@tannerJolson
@writtentospeak
www.writtentospeak.com
Spotify, iTunes, Amazon Music, etc: Written to Speak

Photo by: Adam Fricke // www.adamfricke.com

ACKNOWLEDGEMENTS //

Some of these poems appear on pre-released Written to Speak albums "honest thoughts.", "All Things", and "Welcome to the Other Side."

Thank you to Red Horn Coffee and Brew in Cedar Park, Texas for the coffee and beer as I wrote this book.

Thank you to the team at Sword & Swan Media House, especially Brad Malone, John Rasmussen, Timothy Koch, Katherine Begalke, Julianna Shults, and Jane Fryar for helping make this dream become a reality.

Thank you to Sarah Solinski for your wonderful designs and friendship.

Thank you to ACTS Church Lakeline and the ACTS Church Network in Austin, TX for your kind support and constant prayers. It is an honor to be part of your family.

Thank you to the Orlando Magic for teaching me the meaning of heart and hustle.

Thank you to my friends in Orlando, Wisconsin, St. Louis, Nashville, and Austin.

Thank you to my friends who have walked with me as this book was being written. You are written into every poem I've ever penned.

Thank you to Kris Stack. If you didn't tell me to read 'For Us' that night in West Virginia, I would have never started Written to Speak or have written this book.

Thank you to Justin Fricke and Adam Fricke for being my family.
Go Magic.

Thank you to Gabe Kasper for writing the foreword to this book. I'm not sure where I would be without you.

Thank you to all those who forever changed my life for the better at Camp Luther in Three Lakes, Wisconsin.

Thank you to Man Village. You will forever hold a home in my life. And that home is free of bed bugs.

Thank you to Rachel Wheatley, Trevor Kunze, Kyle Willkom, Taylor Jarman, Kelly Eaton, the Flamingos, the A-Team, the Hickey Family, the McCord Family, the Climo Family, the Littmann Family, the Jackson Family, the Doering families, the Grebing Family, and the Frazier Family for your friendship and constant encouragement.

Thank you to dogs for being dogs and to coffee for being coffee.

Thank you to my family and friends who have become family. Your love and kindness continues to amaze me.

Thank you to the Williams family for allowing me to be part of your lives and for letting your Sarah marry someone who calls himself a poet.

Thank you to those who have supported and followed Written to Speak over the last several years.

Thank you to my Tyler and Greta for your support and encouragement.

Thank you to my mom and dad. Without you I wouldn't be here.
And neither would this book. Let's walk down to the Townhouse for breakfast soon.

Thank you to Sarah Olson for editing these poems. Like everything in my life, you make it better.

Thank you for reading this book.
I am honored that you would spend your time with these words.

If you'd like for me to come share poetry and stories at your school, church, conference, or organization, I would love to be there.

Visit **www.writtentospeak.com** to get in touch.

Made in the
USA
Lexington, KY